TOSCANA

teNeues

TOSCANA

Photographs by Rainer Kiedrowski
Text by Helga Schnehagen

teNeues

La Toscana è la regione italiana più famosa. Il paesaggio più ricco di capolavori d'arte e al contempo più artificiale di tutta la Penisola Appenninica è riuscito a conservare, nonostante l'intervento umano, un'armonia che ha un aspetto magicamente naturale.

I capoluoghi di provincia, Arezzo, Grosseto, Livorno, Lucca, Massa, Pisa, Pistoia, Prato e Siena, e il capoluogo di regione, Firenze, presentano orgogliosi i loro capolavori architettonici, scultorei e pittorici che vanno dall'arte romanica al gotico, al rivoluzionario rinascimento e allo sfarzoso barocco. Con gli Etruschi, 2800 anni fa, la Toscana si pose al centro della storia. Questo misterioso popolo dell'antichità ci ha lasciato necropoli eccezionali – e il proprio nome, dalla cui forma latina "Tusci" deriva "Toscana".

Ma anche la campagna, con la sua incantevole bellezza, può senz'altro fare a gara con le città ed i paesi. Collinare per il 67 per cento, montuosa per il 25 e pianeggiante per il restante 8, la Toscana, che ricopre un'area lunga 200 chilometri e larga 100, è soprattutto varia. Ripide si innalzano verso il cielo le Alpi Apuane, immacolate nelle cave di marmo di Carrara. Lungo si estende il litorale, con la sabbia fine della Versilia, gli scogli della Riviera Etrusca, di nuovo pianeggiante e sabbioso in Maremma. Nell'entroterra un alternarsi di boschi e prati: castagni e abeti caratterizzano le alture della Garfagnana e del Mugello, pinete, macchia profumata e pascoli ridenti fiancheggiano la costa della Toscana meridionale.

Ma la caratteristica della Toscana sono le dolci colline, ricoperte di campi, argentei uliveti luccicanti, ombrosi pini, con maestosi viali di cipressi e solitari casolari. Il modo migliore per conoscere questo stupendo paesaggio, con colline ricoperte di vigneti e dominato da castelli, è percorrere tra Firenze e Siena la Via Chiantigiana, attraversando la zona enologica più conosciuta d'Italia. Le Crete a sudest di Siena e le Balze nei pressi di Volterra costituiscono un brullo contrasto al tipico panorama idilliaco toscano – massicce pendici argillose che si pietrificano sotto il sole cocente a formare un paesaggio lunare le prime, tufo che si spacca in imponenti cave le seconde.

Numerosi film hanno reso famosa in tutto il mondo la Toscana, la sua luce e i suoi colori. Chi non vuol farsi rapir via dalla quotidianità da un tramonto sui colli toscani, con le sue mille ombreggiature, non ha alcuna possibilità di sfuggirgli, in nessun posto.

Helga Schnehagen

Tuscany is Italy's most famous region. The landscape on the Apuan peninsula is richest for its art treasures and also the most artistic. Man-made interventions have not stopped the region preserving a sense of harmony that works quite magically, giving an authentic feel.

The region's major cities proudly present their masterpieces in architecture, sculpture and art from Romanesque and Gothic style, to the revolutionary Renaissance and magnificent Baroque: Arezzo, Grosseto, Livorno, Lucca, Massa, Pisa, Pistoia, Prato, Sienna and Florence, the region's capital. Around 2800 years ago, Tuscany became a historical centre under the Etruscans. This mysterious nation from antiquity left behind fabulous necropolises—and the Latin form of "Tusci", from which the name, Tuscany, is derived.

But because of its spellbinding beauty, the countryside can also stage a great contest to the cities and villages. Around 67 per cent of Tuscany is covered by hills, 25 per cent is mountainous and around 8 per cent of the countryside is flat. The region chiefly represents variety, within an area that is around 200 kilometers long and 100 kilometers wide. The Apuan Alps reach straight up to the sky, they are snow-white in the marble quarries near Carrara. The coastline stretches far into the distance, with a fine sandy beach on the Versilia, rocky cliffs on the Etruscan Riviera and flat and sandy in the Maremma region. In the interior, a play of forest and meadows, chestnut trees and fir trees are typical for the hills in the Garfagnana and Mugello regions. Pine forests, sweet scented macchia and lush willows line the southern coast.

Tuscany's trademarks are its rolling hills, lined with fields, silver shimmering olive groves, shady pines and majestic cypress avenues and isolated farms. This picture-book landscape, with its hills covered in vines and castles towering over the plains, is at its most impressive when you travel on the Via Chiantigiana between Florence and Sienna. The route cuts right across Italy's best known wine-growing region. The "Crete" to the south-east of Sienna and the "Balze" near Volterra are in stark contrast to the typically idyllic Tuscan scenery. In some parts of the "Crete" region, the ground is heavy clay that solidifies to a moonscape under the glare of the sun. Other places around the "Balze" are volcanic rock that collapses in dramatic craters.

Scores of films have made Tuscany internationally famous for its light and colors. If you can't leave everyday life behind whilst gazing at the sunset over Tuscan hills, with their thousands of different shades, you can't escape anywhere.

Helga Schnehagen

Die Toskana ist Italiens berühmteste Region. Die an Kunstschätzen reichste und zugleich künstlichste Landschaft der Apennin-Halbinsel hat es geschafft, trotz der Eingriffe von Menschenhand eine Harmonie zu bewahren, die auf geradezu magische Weise ursprünglich wirkt.

Stolz präsentieren die Provinzhauptstädte ihre Meisterwerke der Architektur, Plastik und Malerei von der Romanik und Gotik über die revolutionäre Renaissance bis zum prunkvollen Barock: Arezzo, Grosseto, Livorno, Lucca, Massa, Pisa, Pistoia, Prato, Siena und die Hauptstadt Florenz. Mit den Etruskern rückte die Toskana vor rund 2800 Jahren in den Blickpunkt der Geschichte. Hinterlassen hat dieses rätselhafte Volk der Antike großartige Nekropolen – und seinen Namen, aus dessen lateinischer Form „Tusci" sich die Toskana ableitet.

Doch auch das Land in seiner betörenden Schönheit kann durchaus mit den Städten und Dörfern konkurrieren. Zu 67 Prozent hügelig, zu 25 Prozent bergig und zu acht Prozent eben, bedeutet die Toskana vor allem Vielfalt in einem Gebiet von rund 200 Kilometern Länge und 100 Kilometern Breite. Schroff recken sich die Apuanischen Alpen gen Himmel, schneeweiß in den Marmorbrüchen bei Carrara. Lang erstreckt sich die Küste, mit feinkörnigem Strand an der Versilia, felsig an der Etruskischen Riviera, wieder flach und sandig in der Maremma. Im Hinterland ein Wechsel von Wald und Wiesen: Kastanien und Tannen charakterisieren die Höhen der Garfagnana und des Mugello, Pinienwälder, duftende Macchia und saftige Weiden säumen die Südküste.

Markenzeichen der Toskana aber sind die sanften Hügel, überzogen von Feldern, silbrig flimmernden Olivenhainen, schattigen Pinien, majestätischen Zypressenalleen und einsamen Gehöften. Am eindrucksvollsten zu erleben ist diese Bilderbuchlandschaft bei einer Fahrt auf der Via Chiantigiana zwischen Florenz und Siena. Mit Hügeln voller Rebstöcke, von Burgen überragt, führt sie mitten durch Italiens bekannteste Weinregion. Karger Kontrast zur typisch toskanischen Idylle sind die Crete südöstlich von Siena und die Balze bei Volterra – hier schwerer Lehmboden, der unter der Sonnenglut zur Mondlandschaft erstarrt, dort Tuffgestein, das in dramatischen Abbrüchen zerfällt.

Zahlreiche Filme haben die Toskana, ihr Licht und die Farben weltweit bekannt gemacht. Wer sich vom Sonnenuntergang über den toskanischen Hügeln in seinen tausend Schattierungen nicht aus dem Alltag entführen lässt, der entrinnt ihm nirgendwo.

Helga Schnehagen

La Toscane est la région la plus célèbre d'Italie. Cette région des Apennins, la plus riche tant au plan des arts que des paysages, a réussi, en dépit des interventions humaines, à conserver une harmonie qui reste miraculeusement authentique.

C'est avec fierté que les capitales provinciales présentent leurs chefs-d'œuvre d'architecture, de sculpture et de peinture de l'époque romane et gothique, de la renaissance révolutionnaire et de la somptueuse époque baroque : Arezzo, Grosseto, Livourne, Lucques, Massa, Pise, Pistoia, Prato, Sienne, et la capitale, Florence. Avec les Étrusques, la Toscane est entrée dans l'histoire il y a quelque 2 800 ans. Ce peuple mystérieux de l'antiquité a laissé un héritage de nécropoles extraordinaires et son nom latin « Tusci » qui est devenu la Toscane.

Le paysage est d'une beauté subjuguante et peut rivaliser avec les villes et les villages. Avec 67 % de collines, 25 % de montagnes et 8 % de plaines, la Toscane offre les visages les plus divers sur une superficie d'environ 200 km de long et 100 km de large. Les Alpes apuanes se dressent massivement vers le ciel ; elles sont éblouissantes de blancheur dans les carrières de marbre près de Carrare. Sur une côte qui s'étire sur de nombreux kilomètres se succèdent les plages de sable fin de la Versilia, les rochers de la riviera étrusque et la plaine sablonneuse de Maremme. Dans l'arrière-pays, les forêts alternent avec les prairies : les châtaigniers et les sapins mettent en relief les hauteurs de la Garfagnana et de Mugello, les pinèdes, le maquis odorant et les pâturages verdoyants bordent la côte sud.

Mais ce qui caractérise d'abord la Toscane, ce sont ses collines aux formes douces, recouvertes de champs, d'oliveraies aux reflets argentés, de pins qui donnent de l'ombre, d'allées de cyprès majestueuses et de fermes isolées. Ce paysage de rêve avec ses collines de vignobles dominées par des châteaux est particulièrement impressionnant quand on prend la Via Chiantigiana, entre Florence et Sienne, qui traverse la région vinicole la plus connue d'Italie. Le « Crete », au sud-est de Sienne, et les falaises des « Balze » près de Volterra contrastent fortement avec la douceur idyllique de la Toscane : ici, des massifs argileux qui se transforment en paysage lunaire sous l'ardeur du soleil, là, des formations de tuf accidentées et tourmentées.

Nombreux sont les films qui ont fait connaître la Toscane, sa lumière et ses couleurs dans le monde entier. Sans oublier les prodigieux couchers de soleil sur les collines de la Toscane auxquels il est difficile de rester insensible.

Helga Schnehagen

La Toscana es la región más famosa de Italia. El paisaje más rico en tesoros artísticos y, al mismo tiempo, más artificial de la Península de los Apeninos ha conseguido, a pesar de las intervenciones de la mano del hombre, conservar una armonía que, de una manera casi mágica, parece natural.

Las capitales de la provincia presentan orgullosas sus obras maestras de la arquitectura, escultura y pintura desde el Románico y el Gótico pasando por el revolucionario Renacimiento hasta el Barroco fastuoso: Arezzo, Grosseto, Livorno, Lucca, Massa, Pisa, Pistoia, Prato, Siena y la capital Florencia. Con los Etruscos, hace alrededor de 2800 años, la Toscana se convirtió en el punto de mira de la historia. Este pueblo enigmático de la Antigüedad legó grandiosas necrópolis –y su nombre de cuya forma latina "Tusci" se deriva la Toscana.

Pero también la campaña, en su embriagadora belleza, puede competir absolutamente con las ciudades y pueblos. En un 67 por ciento con colinas, en un 25 por ciento montañosa y en un 8 por ciento llana, la Toscana significa sobre todo variedad en un territorio de alrededor de 200 kilómetros de longitud y 100 kilómetros de anchura. Los Alpes de Apuania se estiran escarpados hacia el cielo, blancos por la nieve en las canteras de mármol cerca de Carrara. La costa se extiende larga, con una playa de arena fina en Versilia, rocosa en la Riviera Etrusca y nuevamente lisa y arenosa en Maremma. En el interior, una alternancia de bosques y praderas: Los castaños y los abetos caracterizan las colinas de Garfagnana y de Mugello, los pinares, los matorrales olorosos y los jugosos sauces bordean la costa del sur.

Pero la marca característica de la Toscana son las suaves colinas cubiertas de campos, los olivares de un relucir plateado, los pinos dando sombra, las majestuosas avenidas de cipreses y las granjas solitarias. La manera más impresionante de vivir este paisaje de película con colinas llenas de cepas y dominado por castillos es viajando por la Via Chiantigiana, entre Florencia y Siena, que conduce a través de la región vinícola más famosa de Italia. Un árido contraste con el típico idilio toscano son Crete, al sudeste de Siena, y Balze, cerca de Volterra –aquí un duro suelo arcilloso que bajo el ardor del sol se solidifica como un paisaje lunar, allí tobas que se desmoronan derrumbándose dramáticamente.

Numerosas películas han hecho mundialmente famosa a la Toscana, su luz y sus colores. Quien no se deja secuestrar de la rutina por la puesta de sol sobre las colinas toscanas en sus miles de matices, no se escapará de ella en ninguna parte.

Helga Schnehagen

Front cover: Da San Quirico d'Órcia
Back cover: Pisa, Val d'Órcia, Parco Naturale della
Maremma, San Gimignano

Photographs © 2003 Rainer Kiedrowski
© 2004 teNeues Verlag GmbH + Co. KG, Kempen
All rights reserved.

Rainer Kiedrowski
Peddenkamp 64
40883 Ratingen
Phone: 0049-(0)2102-66593
Fax: 0049-(0)2102-69922
e-mail: bildarchiv@photo-kiedrowski.de
www.photo-kiedrowski.de

Photographs by Rainer Kiedrowski
Design by Axel Theyhsen
Introduction by Helga Schnehagen
Translation by SWB Communications,
Dr. Sabine Werner-Birkenbach, Mainz
Dr. Nicoletta Negri (Italian)
Dr. Suzanne Kirkbright (English)
Dominique Le Pluart (French)
Gemma Correa-Buján (Spanish)
Editorial coordination by Sabine Wagner
Production by Dieter Haberzettl
Color separation by Medien Team-Vreden, Germany

While we strive for utmost precision in every detail,
we cannot be held responsible for any inaccuracies,
neither for any subsequent loss or damage arising.

Bibliographic information published by Die Deutsche
Bibliothek. Die Deutsche Bibliothek lists this publica-
tion in the Deutsche Nationalbibliographie; detailed
bibliographic data is available in the Internet at
http://dnb.ddb.de

ISBN 3-8238-4567-5

Printed in Italy

teNeues Publishing Group
Kempen
Düsseldorf
London
Madrid
New York
Paris

Published by teNeues Publishing Group

teNeues Book Division
Kaistraße 18
40221 Düsseldorf
Germany
Phone: 0049-(0)211-99 45 97-0
Fax: 0049-(0)211-99 45 97-40
e-mail: books@teneues.de
Press department: arehn@teneues.de
Phone: 0049-(0)2152-916-202

teNeues Publishing Company
16 West 22nd Street
New York, N.Y. 10010
USA
Phone: 001-212-627-9090
Fax: 001-212-627-9511

teNeues Publishing UK Ltd.
P.O. Box 402
West Byfleet
KT14 7ZF
Great Britain
Phone: 0044-1932-403509
Fax: 0044-1932-403514

teNeues France S.A.R.L.
4, rue de Valence
75005 Paris
France
Phone: 0033-1-55 76 62 05
Fax: 0033-1-55 76 64 19

www.teneues.com

teNeues